MARYLAND A PORTRAIT

Robin Levin, Photographer

IMAGE PUBLISHING, LTD.

IMAGE PUBLISHING, LTD.
1411 Hollins Street/Union Square
410 • 566-1222   Baltimore, Maryland 21223   FAX 410 • 233-1241

CREDITS
Photography by Roger Miller
Design by David Miller
Text by Ron Pilling
Text edited by Bonnie L. Baer
Text coordinated by Sarah C. Carter
Text revised by Margaretta H. Finn
Phototypesetting revised by Delta Graphics, Inc.
Printing, color separations and binding by Everbest Printing Co., Ltd., Hong Kong
Printing Agent Four Colour Imports, Ltd., Louisville, Kentucky

INFORMATION

Library of Congress Catalog Card Number: 86-081383 (1st. edition)
Library of Congress Catalog Card Number: 88-081950 (revised edition)

ISBN 0-911897-02-X HARD COVER
ISBN 0-911897-12-7 SOFT COVER

First Printing 1986, Second Printing 1988, Third Printing 1990, Fourth Printing 1992.
Printed in Hong Kong.

ORDER
For direct orders please call or write for specific cost and postage and handling to the above address. Discounts available for stores and institutions, minimum orders required.

DEDICATION
Adrienne Monninger-Miller
I am proud to dedicate this book to my new daughter, Adrienne. Born May 4, 1986. I pray she is able to see and enjoy a state even more beautiful than we have now.

Roger Miller, 6-6-86

I can't believe that I have learned so much from her!

Roger Miller, 7-7-88

SPECIAL THANKS
I would like to thank everyone who had a part in this project. I would especially like to thank the following:

A special thanks to all the people and businesses of Maryland. Without their hard work and dedication to making Maryland the great state it is, this book would not have been possible.

I would like to thank **Governor William Donald Schaefer** for his invaluable assistance in writing the foreword to "Maryland A Portrait."

For their efforts and belief in this project I would like to thank everyone at **NCNB of Maryland** particularly **Lee Boatwright, Mike Glump,** and **Gail Houser.** NCNB is truly a bank which believes in the people and the state of Maryland.

For their help and assistance I would like to thank all the people in Economic Development and Tourism Offices around the state.

A very special thanks to **Wayne Chapell,** Executive Director of the Baltimore Convention Bureau, for his friendship, foresight and commitment to new ideas to promote both Baltimore and Maryland.

I would like to thank my dedicated staff for putting up with some of the pressure we have dealt with in creating our books. Without the efforts and devotion of **Bonnie L. Baer, Sarah C. Carter** and **Margaretta H. Finn** this book would not exist.

Roger Miller

MARYLAND A PORTRAIT

Photography by Roger Miller

Text by Ron Pilling **Foreword by William Donald Schaefer** **Design and Editing by David Miller**

Chesapeake Bay at Kent Island

CONTENTS

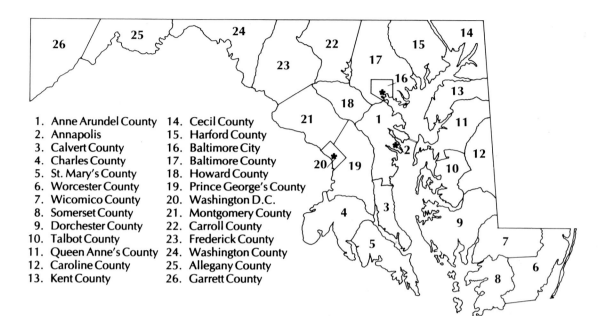

William Donald Schaefer on the Baltimore and Annapolis Railway.

FOREWORD

I have lived in Maryland all of my life and have had the privilege and pleasure of visiting many of its scenic beauties. The allure and magnetism of its attractions are boundless. A lifetime is virtually not enough time to see all that Maryland has to offer.

Maryland is a state rich in heritage that speaks to our aspirations for an even greater tomorrow. It is a constant series of changing phases and events. A state that is bountiful with all of Nature's beauty. A place to take great pleasure in the achievements of the past and a place to look forward to the vision of the future.

For more than three and a half centuries men and women have worked to make Maryland a better state. Just as they are working today to make it a better place for the future. The story of Maryland abounds with tales of courage, accounts of hard work, and tragedies of fighting. Maryland is steeped in narratives of joy, dramas of sadness and sagas of men and women who performed wise deeds and of a few who made mistakes.

As a buff of Maryland history and a longtime elected public servant directing and overseeing the day-to-day activities of a major metropolitan area, I never cease to be amazed at the foresight of our earliest ancestors.

When they boarded the "Ark" and the "Dove" on a crisp November morning in 1633, they were prepared for life in the new colony. Stored aboard the ships were great sacks and barrels of flour, jugs of vinegar, and pounds of dried meat, butter, salt, rice, oats and peas.

Also amassed were boxes of soap and bedding and chests of clothes. Nails and tools for building houses and boats were not forgotten. Dogs, guns, powder and bullets were brought along for protection and hunting. Fishing lines and nets for catching fish were in abundance.

Also on board were shipbuilders, carpenters, blacksmiths, bricklayers and farmers. When the colonies of Virginia and Plymouth were founded, many settlers died from hunger and cold. One of the best parts of Lord Baltimore's plan was that voyagers would reach Maryland in the spring. This would give them plenty of time to build houses and to plant and harvest crops before winter set in. With this advanced planning, there is little wonder that the colony of Maryland was off to a good start.

From these sturdy beginnings the colony and the state flourished. The settlers found that contained within the colony were the magnificent Chesapeake Bay, flowing trout streams, blue-ridged mountains, grottoes and caverns, and the whole area was blooming and abounding with wildflowers and wildlife.

Today those same attractions still exist. Now with the additions and refinements made through the years by our forefathers - the allure is even greater.

The Maryland of today contains hospitals that are the pride of the nation and battlefields where liberty was fought for and won. Picturesque covered bridges, lighthouses, and tidewater plantation houses surrounded by fields of rippling tobacco still grace the landscape. Whole areas of the state contain truck farm after truck farm blossoming with tomatoes, corn, cantaloupes and watermelons. There is the Cumberland Narrows where you can walk with generations past as they marched westward to forge this nation.

I mention these attractions for several reasons. Tourism today is one of the three largest industries in the state of Maryland. Leading authorities predict that by the year 2000—tourism will be the largest industry in the world.

In a decade and a half as Mayor of the City of Baltimore I have been privileged to have received numerous accolades. One major publication referred to me "as the driving force behind the transformation of an aging port, city into a sparkling showcase for tourism, cultural activities and urban rejuvenation."

For many years Baltimore was a city to pass through—as quickly as possible—on your way to New York or D.C. But that has all changed. People now go out of their way to come to Baltimore. They come from every state in the nation and every continent on the globe. And they come by the millions.

Strange as it may seem, new buildings and attractions are only symbols of a city's growth—not the growth itself. Growth must be felt. There must be a feeling among the people. They must be willing to put their efforts toward it. Baltimore is growing and enjoying the infusion of dream weavers. Citizens are proud of themselves and of their heritage.

Several years ago I was down at Baltimore's Inner Harbor for the final night of the City Fair—where the city gathers to look at itself and the neighborhoods renew their separate identities. The Baltimore Symphony Orchestra was playing the "1812 Overture" and at the appropriate time the guns roared out from Federal Hill. Fireworks lighted up the sky. And the clipper ship, "Pride of Baltimore", under full sail, glided smoothly and gracefully across the waters of the Inner Harbor. And an elderly lady in the audience—with tears streaming down her cheeks said, "Baltimore, you're getting to be too much."

I see this sense of pride throughout the entire state. I would call it cultural vitality—the sum of the concepts and beliefs, the skill and the habits and the institutions of a people. It is the work characteristics of a neighborhood, city, town, population or state. It is cultural heritage. It is the architecture and the structure. It is conservation and preservation. It is a major social, economic and environmental force affecting visitors and residents alike.

In the following pages Roger Miller has captured Maryland through the lens of his camera. History becomes alive! Beauty becomes enhanced! Living and working become real! Relaxing becomes a fantasy! And people show up as themselves—honest, genuine people! Roger has captured a memory and given a vision of a future.

William Donald Schaefer

The Maryland Dove, St. Mary's City

INTRODUCTION

It is early 1632, in a manor house in the north of England. Three brothers, Leonard, Philip, and Cecilius Calvert are planning the colonization of a large piece of land in the New World. North of the Potomac River, the new colony had been granted by the Crown to their late father, George, First Lord Baltimore. They will name it "Maryland", after the king's wife, Henrietta Maria.

Maryland; She is the fruit of all the Calvert's dreams, the years of their loyal service to King James I, and the worthy intentions of the proprietors. For three-and-a-half centuries, Maryland has stood true to the Calverts' expectations. It is a land that offers great opportunity to its natives, a state as diverse as the settlers it welcomed in its earliest days.

But sitting around a table in Yorkshire in 1632, the proprietors could have had no idea of the eventual scale of their project. Since its auspicious beginnings, Maryland has fondly been called "America in Miniature", referring to the diverse geography. In fact, Maryland mirrors the entire nation in more ways than simply its terrain. In the 350 years since settlers first landed, Marylanders have developed a multi-faceted economy and have made significant contributions to every important industry in the country.

So today some of us still earn a living oystering or crabbing as generations before have done. Others work in aerospace, data communications, or medical technology. Maryland fosters an environment that has helped the growth of firms whose trademarks are known across America: McCormick Spices, Noxzema, Martin-Marietta, and Perdue Foods, among others.

The climate is friendly, almost temperate in the south: There is a landscape to suit almost anyone. The Atlantic beaches are as fine as those anywhere on the East Coast. In the Maryland midsection, the rolling fields are reminiscent of the blue grass of Kentucky. Southern Maryland's sprawling flatlands have the slow, friendly ambiance of the South. Maryland's mountainous west blends the modern amenities of the ski resort with the spirit of the pioneers.

When the first settlers landed on St. Clement's Island on March 25, 1634, however, it would be a century before the western reaches of the colony would be opened. A colony had to be planted first. For the Lords Baltimore, colonization was not simply a means to accumulate wealth, for they had different ideas about the new society they would eventually build on the shores of the Chesapeake Bay. Their first priority, a concept unheard of in Seventeenth Century England, was to create a free colony in which people of all denominations could live in peace and harmony. The Calverts were Roman Catholics, and thus accustomed to religious persecution.

There were pressing tasks to be faced in those early days. Farmland was as yet unplowed and there was no formal political organization. Nonetheless, the colony prospered from the start. Calvert had planned the voyage so that the colonists arrived in the spring. A large supply of food accompanied them and farmers were encouraged to grow subsistence crops rather than only tobacco. Within the first year of settlement a legislative assembly had met. The Toleration Act of 1649 guaranteed the freedom of religious choice that had been George Calvert's dream.

Though Maryland had a promising start it was not without its difficulties. Life was hard and relations with Virginia were unstable. It took a short war between the neighboring colonies in 1635 to bring about a decision by the Crown regarding the boundary. Other political disputes had an impact on the fledgling settlement. The Civil War in England caused disruption of normal colonial life. It was not until 1689 that politics stabilized and order returned.

Growth could then proceed. The abundance of food, coupled with the easy conditions on which land was granted and the religious toleration that prevailed led to a rapidly-increasing population. As settlements began to spread from St. Mary's northward other counties were formed: Kent in 1642, Anne Arundel in 1650, Calvert in 1654, Charles in 1658. The state capital moved to Annapolis in 1695. By the close of the Seventeenth Century the Maryland map had been neatly divided from Baltimore east to the ocean.

Maryland moved steadily through the early 1700's. Baltimore was founded in 1729 as a commercial center. The population increased rapidly, and by the time of the Revolution 250 thousand colonists called Maryland home. Maryland was almost wholly agricultural, tobacco being the chief crop although wheat was grown in the central and western valleys. Life in Southern Maryland was much like that on plantations throughout the South. Much of that southern ambiance still exists.

On the Eastern Shore, the Chesapeake Bay set the pace for the general economy, and in Maryland's midlands large fields of wheat dotted the landscape, much as today. In the mountains to the west Maryland pioneers had begun to hew a civilization out of the wilderness by the French and Indian War in 1754. Frederick was laid out in 1745, Hagerstown in 1752, and as early as 1755 there was a fort at Cumberland.

At the same time, a certain spirit was spreading throughout the English colonies, a spirit that would take Maryland headlong into the Revolution. The "Old Line State" sent five representatives to the Continental Congresses and the colony assumed a leadership role in these formative years. Charles Carroll (reputedly the richest man in America when he put his name to the Declaration of Independence) added the postscript "of Carrollton" to his signature so that King George would not confuse him with his cousin of the same name.

Maryland troops performed with courage. At the Battle of Long Island, our soldiers held off an immensely superior British force under Lord Cornwallis. They went on to sustain the reputation they had earned in the war's early days. By the war's close, the troops of the Maryland Line had participated in nearly every major campaign.

Garrett County

In the halls of Congress Marylanders made equally important contributions. Thomas Johnson, later the first governor of the state, nominated George Washington to be Commander-in-Chief of the army. For a time, Baltimore was the seat of Congress. At the close of the war, Annapolis became the temporary national capital. In proportion to her size and population, Maryland bore more than her share of the Revolution's burdens.

The period between the Revolution and the War of 1812 was one of enormous growth for the state. Grain exports made Baltimore a boom town, and the population there grew from 8,000 in 1782 to 25,000 by 1800.

Peace brought about a resumption of cultural and social life and a renewed interest in education. Washington College in Chestertown was founded in 1782, St. John's College in Annapolis opened its doors in 1784, and in 1785 the University of Maryland was formed.

While the state was prospering its leading citizens participated in the formation of the national union. Marylander John Hanson served as the first President "of the United States in Congress Assembled" under the Articles of Confederation. When it was obvious that the loose confederation would be inadequate, Maryland led the way to the Constitutional Convention, hosting the first meeting toward that end in Annapolis in 1786.

But the good times were to be threatened by the second war with Great Britain, fought for commercial freedom - a cause dear to the hearts of Marylanders. This time the state was a battleground. In 1813 many small bay-side towns were bombarded when the British captured Washington and sent its leaders fleeing into the Maryland countryside.

A year later British Admiral Cockburn returned, landing troops at North Point outside Baltimore. The plan was to pinch the "nest of pirates" between his land forces and the battleships bombarding Fort McHenry at the mouth of the harbor. Baltimore clippers were wreaking havoc against British shipping as far away as the Mediterranean, and Cockburn wanted to put a stop to the privateering trade. As Francis Scott Key described in "The Star-Spangled Banner", Cockburn failed. The fort and the city endured a 24-hour siege throughout the 13th of September, 1814. Before the end of the year peace was signed, and Maryland could get back to the work of economic development and expansion.

Her first task was to build the roads and canals that would enable trade to grow, and the direction was westward. Baltimore was the third largest port in America by 1815 and the closest port to wilderness cities like Pittsburgh. Maryland was the gateway to the West. The Chesapeake and Ohio Canal was completed from Georgetown, near Washington, to Cumberland by 1830. On the 4th of July, 1828, Charles Carroll of Carrollton laid the cornerstone for the Baltimore and Ohio Railroad, undoubtedly the most important commercial event of the century. Maryland pioneered rail travel in the United States, and economic progress continued unabated until the Civil War.

The controversy over slavery flared in Maryland, for no other state occupied a more difficult position. Secession talk was strong, but the federal capital lay within her borders. Maryland took a prudent course, choosing to remain in the Union though many of her citizens joined the Southern cause either in their hearts or with their arms.

Once again the state would see blood spilled in battle. In April of 1861 there was a riot in Baltimore that resulted in the first bloodshed of the war. In September of 1863 the calm around the rural town of Sharpsburg in Washington County was shattered. The Battle of Antietam, named for the creek that flowed near Sharpsburg, resulted in more casualties than any other single-day battle in the war. Today's landscape around the still-quiet burg is dotted with monuments to the 25,000 who fell there.

Fortunately, the close of the Civil War brought renewed prosperity and steady economic growth. A new state constitution was proposed in 1864 which abolished slavery and in 1867 it passed, laying the groundwork for a powerful assembly which still works hand-in-hand with private enterprise.

Much of the state returned to life as it had been for centuries. Soldiers returned to the tobacco fields of Southern Maryland and to the oyster beds of the Chesapeake Bay. Ex-infantrymen and cavalrymen harvested wheat in Carroll County and returned to the logging trails and coal mines of the mountains. But for Baltimore, the picture began to change rapidly.

The post-Civil War years in "The Monumental City" were years of unprecedented economic boom. In the late 1800's railroads spread from Baltimore to every major city in the nation, and Baltimoreans grew rich. Grain, canned goods, cattle, copper, and tobacco were exported in record amounts while coffee, fruits, iron ore, and chemicals came into the port. In 1865 a new City Hall was built and was shortly thereafter dwarfed by new buildings springing up in every direction. A devastating fire that destroyed much of the downtown in 1904 proved to be nothing more than a stumbling block in Baltimore's relentless march toward prosperity.

Much of this new-found wealth made its way back to the community. This was the era of great philanthropy: Peabody Institute opened in 1866, Johns Hopkins University was founded in 1876, the Enoch Pratt Free Library in 1882.

Baltimore and the state have continued their prominence in national affairs and development ever since. As monuments on village and town squares all over the state testify, Marylanders fought bravely in both World Wars, Korea, and Vietnam. Our industries have rallied to the nation's call, notably the Glenn L. Martin Company in the production of airplanes and the massive Bethlehem Steel plant at Sparrows Point.

In the process, the economic face of the state has changed. The economy is no longer strictly agricultural, though our earliest industries of farming, fishing, and mining are still important. Baltimore is the home of many important manufacturing concerns whose labels are known across the nation. The area around Washington is home to many high technology industries involved in data processing, communications, medicine, and space research and development. As the United States has grown, so has the economic scope of the Free State.

As the myriad charms and wonders of Maryland are discovered tourism has become a more important industry. The renaissance of downtown Baltimore, focused on the bright Inner Harbor, now attracts tens of thousands of visitors per year who, a decade ago, never heard of the city. The boom in tourism has spread to other parts of the state as well. More guests than ever enjoy the beaches of Ocean City, sail the waters of the Chesapeake Bay, or ski the slopes of Garrett County.

We hope that this state portrait encourages you to get out and see more of what Maryland has to offer. No matter where in our fair state you wander we can safely make this promise: It will be more than you can imagine.

The Chesapeake Bay from Point Lookout, St. Mary's County

SOUTHERN MARYLAND

Captain John Smith was the first European to explore the lower watershed of the Potomac and Patuxent Rivers. He wrote in his ship's log that the area was "fruitful and delightsome" when he sailed there in 1607.

Today, Navy planes from the Patuxent Naval Air Test Center fly daily over the same waters, covering the same distance in minutes that took Captain Smith days in his small ship. Obviously much has changed in southern Maryland in the past 350 years. But then again, much has remained the same.

There are no colossal tourist magnets here—no Ocean City, no Baltimore Inner Harbor. Perhaps that is why southern Maryland is such a well-kept secret, even among Marylanders. All most people know of the region is what they recall from the old "one-armed bandit" days, when slot machines in every motel lobby, restaurant, bar, and lunch stand in Waldorf attracted veteran gamblers. Those days are gone, but the best of southern Maryland remains.

Fields of tobacco still blanket much of the landscape—but the farmers have turned to computers to help them grow and market their product. Fishermen still set out from Solomons Island, Chesapeake Beach, and other coastal villages for oysters, crabs, and bluefish—but now work in concert with state officials in a monumental modern effort to clean the environment so that watermen can work the Bay for many generations to come. Many southern Marylanders do the same work as their forebears have for hundreds of years. Others work on sophisticated radar systems at Westinghouse, or man the Calvert Cliffs Nuclear Power Plant in Calvert County.

The terrain is flat, broken only by an occasional farm silo or a stand of tall pines. Seldom is one far from water. Southern Maryland boasts the state's longest growing period, and though agriculture is a major factor in the local economy, business is more diverse than one would expect at first glance. People come here to work, but as many come here to play. Camping, boating, fishing—anything that can be done on the water is popular.

Because of its proximity to Baltimore and Washington, Anne Arundel County is the most populous subdivision of southern Maryland, and major employers are concentrated here. High technology industry flourishes, with pioneering firms in electronics, communications, data processing, and weaponry calling Anne Arundel County home.

Today, the seat of Maryland political power is in Annapolis, the state capital since 1695. Annapolis is the gem of southern Maryland. Sitting at the confluence of the Severn River and the Chesapeake Bay, the town occupies three peninsulas and has a 16-mile waterfront. Arguably the state's most sophisticated city, Annapolis puts forward a facade of unhurried life. Yet under the surface politics seethes. Lobbyists work every restaurant and night spot feverishly while the legislature is in session.

Annapolis is warm and inviting and maybe a bit conceited. Its shop windows are filled with the Annapolis uniform: wool suits for men and women in the winter and jaunty yachting apparel for the warm months. The small city invites you to sit by the water at harborside, watching sailboats bound for the Chesapeake Bay beyond while enjoying local specialties at a dockside eatery. Its restored homes and public buildings depict life in the eighteenth century, but the underlying feeling is not that of a museum, but of a hard-working modern city.

Its hub is at the Market House, on the small city harbor. Automobile traffic swirls rapidly around the market building, the only disturbance in what is otherwise a charming setting. Around the harbor are clusters of shops, galleries and restaurants. The narrow streets that end here wind their way up the hill to the historic State House, St. John's College, and Church Circle.

Annapolis is one of the most pristinely-kept colonial cities in America. It is filled with important residences. Some, including the Chase-Lloyd House, the William Paca House, and the Hammond-Harwood House were homes of prominent early Marylanders. The city's charm, however, lies in its streets of narrow, clapboard rowhouses that were built for the artisans and watermen who made up Annapolis's colonial middle class.

The existence of so many historic buildings testifies to the success of Historic Annapolis, Inc. and the Historic District Commission. The former realized the historic importance of the city long before there were tax breaks for those saving old buildings from demolition—long before "preservation" was fashionable. Historic Annapolis now sponsors walking tours in addition to its efforts to guarantee the future of Annapolis's past.

While most Annapolitans left their tiny homes each morning for shops near the wharf or the Chesapeake Bay itself, important decisions have been made in and around State Circle at the top of the hill. The 1772 State House has been the scene of urgent debate, its leaders participating in nearly every event that fills American history books. The Continental Congress met here in 1783 when George Washington resigned his commission—an act that set the stage for 200 years of American democracy. The following year, in these same halls, Congress ratified the Treaty of Paris, officially ending the Revolution.

Maryland has a bicameral legislature that meets in Annapolis the first three months of every year. Maryland's Governor makes his home in Government House, built on State Circle in 1869. During the legislative session Annapolis is much as it must have been during sessions of the court in colonial days. The hotels are packed with out-of-town visitors, the taverns and restaurants are filled to overflowing.

Undoubtedly it was the town's special location that led to the opening of the

St. Mary's County farmlands

14

United States Naval Academy in Annapolis in 1845. The Navy defended the country under sail in those days, and what better place to train sailors than the Chesapeake Bay? The Academy has left its mark on the city ever since, and at times Annapolis seems more like a college town than a state capital. Sunday afternoons find hundreds of midshipmen in their distinctive whites strolling the streets with their families.

What appealed to the Navy also offers special benefits to the yachting set, making Annapolis one of the East Coast's major sailing centers. From any of the bridges crossing Spa Creek, the Severn River, or the nearby South River motorists can look across the water to forests of masts bobbing at shoreline marinas. From the Chesapeake Bay Bridge on a sunny day the water is blanketed by bright white sails. Sailing associations sponsor regattas and races, and there are several schools to introduce the novice to the sailing world.

For those content to sit back and let someone else tend the helm, there are harbor cruises, trips from the harbor across the Bay to St. Michael's, and plenty of sailboat charters. A stroll along the wharf any summer evening takes one past moored sailboats, many with signs tied in their shrouds announcing their availability for charter or for luxurious cruises.

Annapolis is in some respects the center of life in Maryland, yet one can't help but get the feeling that the city is somehow detached from the rest of the state. Its appearance is of the eighteenth century and the lifestyle that it puts forth to the public—sailing, lounging at the sidewalk cafes—is dramatically different from the rest of the Old Line State. Yet there could be no more appropriate setting for the state capital than this waterfront town. Here Maryland's heritage is on the surface for all to see, her past is an obvious guide to direct her future.

Route 2, south from Annapolis, covers fifty miles and two centuries. The underlying bustle of Annapolis quickly drops away as one heads south into Calvert County. Nestled between the Bay on the east and the Patuxent River to the west, it is water that sets the pace here. The county economy is closely-linked to its maritime heritage. Baltimore Gas and Electric Company is the county's largest employer at its nuclear plant, but a review of Calvert County's other companies exposes its watery perspective. Fiberglass boats are built here, masts and rigging are turned out, and seafood is harvested, processed, and sent from Calvert County all over the eastern seaboard.

At Calvert County's very tip, in the village of Solomons, is the Calvert Maritime Museum. Much here speaks of the past. A seafood-packer's shed has been rebuilt and the 1883 Drum Point Lighthouse stands sentinel. But displays of marine biological studies and explanations of the work of twentieth century scientists makes it plain that Calvert County has no intention of ignoring its future. Calvert is a county that is dedicated to maintaining its centuries-old maritime connection while safeguarding the future of the waters that surround it.

A short drive across the bridge over the Patuxent from Solomons leads to St. Mary's County. It all began here, when the Ark and the Dove landed near St. Mary's City in 1634. St Mary's County is as far south-both geographically and culturally—as one can get in Maryland. The pace is slower than to the north, the economy more tightly connected to the land. The landscape is dotted with tobacco barns with their distinctive slotted walls to allow air to circulate around the drying tobacco within. Farmers meet at the corner stores, discussing produce prices and comparing modern agricultural techniques. Every third vehicle on the narrow country roads seems to be a pick-up. The distinctive drone of the tobacco auctioneer can be heard throughout the county in the springtime.

In St. Mary's County, a firm with 100 workers on the payroll is a major employer. But this doesn't mean that the county is an economic backwater. Local firms produce electronic devices and computer systems. The Patuxent Naval Air Test Center is the county's largest employer. The museum here testifies to St. Mary's County's role in developing sophisticated aircraft.

Visitors come here first for history, and discover the county's unknown charms only after paying homage to our past at the reconstructed State House in St. Mary's City. Down here in southern Maryland things aren't discarded simply because they are old. As a result, the county is a treasure-trove of historic houses and churches. In Leonardtown, the county seat, the old jail has been converted into a museum. At Coltons Point there is a museum dedicated to 17th century Indian and colonial culture. Monuments throughout the county mark the sites of our earliest history.

Just to the north, in Charles County, the pace is quicker and the landscape is proof. Waldorf is but 22 miles from the national capital, and as the Washington metro area has grown Charles County has followed suit. Developers have built suburban communities as fast here as in any other place in Maryland. For example, St. Charles, south of Waldorf, is a completely new town built in response to this residential boom.

Both bureaucrats and businesses have found Charles County to be a perfect home. Local firms in the dairy industry, building materials, and publishing keep the county's unemployment rate the lowest in the region. There are no enormous corporations here, just a diverse collection of dozens of successful, small concerns.

Heading south, away from Capitol Hill, one quickly sees the familiar sights of southern Maryland. Tobacco farms abound and tractors hug the shoulders of the farm lanes. Fresh produce is sold every Saturday at the Farmers' Market in the county seat, LaPlata. Its sister market, in nearby Charlotte Hall, offers produce, antiques, and a country flea market every Saturday and Wednesday year-round. Amish farmers and their families man many of the market's stalls.

Like much of the rest of southern Maryland, history is not far beneath the surface of Charles County. To the north the county seems intent on streaking into the 21st Century, but the many historic sites in the south remind county residents of their past. Some of Maryland's finest old homes are here: Friendship House, dating from 1658, is on the grounds of the Charles County Community College near LaPlata. In Smallwood State Park the home of General William Smallwood, Revolutionary patriot, is open to guests.

A long weekend cruising the roads from Annapolis south to St. Mary's is barely enough to uncover the secrets of southern Maryland. Much here is reminiscent of the more popular Eastern Shore. The pace of life is a bit old-fashioned. The hearty cuisine relies on local products from the waters of the Bay and area's farms. Anything one enjoys on the water one can find here. The only thing missing is the crowds.

ANNE ARUNDEL COUNTY

Since the state capital moved to Annapolis, Anne Arundel County has been the focal point of much Maryland activity—cultural and economic as well as political. With its past firmly anchored in Maryland history, the county offers economic opportunity as well as excellent recreational facilities to its residents and guests.

THE STATE HOUSE

With a fine hilltop prospect of the entire town of Annapolis, the Maryland State House has been in continuous use since 1772. The Old Senate Chamber is restored to its colonial appearance. The capital's dome, completed in 1788, is the largest wooden dome in the U.S.

GOVERNMENT HOUSE
First built in Victorian style and later remodeled in Georgian fashion, Government House has been home to Maryland's governors since 1869.

St. John's College

ST. JOHN'S COLLEGE

St. John's College in Annapolis traces its beginnings to King William's School, one of America's first public schools opened in 1696. On the lawn is a huge tulip poplar, the "Liberty Tree", under which a 1652 treaty with the Indians was signed. The college is an ancient and important Annapolis landmark.

Paca House and Gardens

PACA HOUSE AND GARDENS

William Paca, one of Maryland's representatives on the Declaration of Independence, built this elegant Annapolis home in 1765. It has been snatched from the jaws of developers many times in its history and is now one of the state's finest restored colonial residences.

The Paca House is nearly eclipsed by the grandeur of its extensive gardens. The herb garden, holly, rose, and boxwood plantings are based on an early painting of Mr. Paca in the rear of his mansion.

Paca House Interior

St. Anne's Church

Chase-Lloyd House

Hammond-Harwood House

CHASE-LLOYD HOUSE

Another Maryland signer of the Declaration of Independence, Samuel Chase, began this Annapolis home in 1769. It was completed by a state governor, Edward Lloyd and features fine interior woodwork.

HAMMOND-HARWOOD HOUSE

The Hammond-Harwood House in Annapolis has been called one of the finest Georgian homes in America. It was planned and built by William Buckland, a premier American colonial architect.

ST. ANNE'S CHURCH

The first church was built on Church Circle in Annapolis in the late 1600's. The present St. Anne's dates from 1858. Sir Robert Eden, the last colonial governor of Maryland, is buried in the church yard.

Graduation Week, United States Naval Academy in Annapolis

Preble Hall, USNA

Midshipmen, USNA

Bancroft Hall, USNA

United States Naval Academy, Chapel

UNITED STATES NAVAL ACADEMY

In 1845 the United States Naval Academy was established in Annapolis. Of interest to visitors here is the final resting place of John Paul Jones, and the USNA maritime museum in Preble Hall. Bancroft Hall, site of daily brigade formations, is the midshapmen's dormitory. Dominating the grounds is the United States Naval Academy Chapel, where Jones is interred.

Sailing on the Chesapeake

Annapolis Harbor

Broome's Island

CALVERT COUNTY

Calvert County, in southern Maryland, is sandwiched between the Chesapeake Bay and the Patuxent River. As could be expected, much of its economy is based on the water. Nature has been generous to Calvert County, and several of its splendid natural features—notably Calvert Cliffs and the Battle Creek Cypress Swamp—are well-known.

BROOM'S ISLAND

From September to March oyster, crab, and fishing boats ply the waters around Broome's Island in Calvert County.

Drum Point Light

DRUM POINT LIGHTHOUSE
Drum Point Lighthouse dominates the Calvert Maritime Museum in Solomons, Calvert County.
Built in 1883, it is one of a few surviving lighthouses in a style that once dotted the entire East Coast.

Calvert Cliffs

CALVERT CLIFFS

Discovered by Captain John Smith in 1608, Calvert Cliffs extends for 30 miles along the Chesapeake Bay. The Cliffs are well-known as an extensive depository of fossils.

Calvert County

Charles County

CHARLES COUNTY

Charles County is in the heart of southern Maryland tobacco country. Agriculture provides income for many county residents whose products are sold in the county's farmers' markets and tobacco auction warehouses.

Southern Maryland is home to a prosperous Amish farming community. Known as excellent farmers and astute businesspeople, the Amish sell their products at several area farmers' markets.

William Smallwood Mansion

WILLIAM SMALLWOOD MANSION

Revolutionary War hero General William Smallwood made his home here, now part of Smallwood State Park in Charles County.

Dr. Samuel Mudd House

DR. SAMUEL MUDD HOUSE

John Wilkes Booth made his escape from Washington following the assassination of Abraham Lincoln through Sothern Maryland in 1865. One stop was at the home of local doctor Samuel Mudd, in Charles County, where Booth had his broken leg set.

Port Tobacco

PORT TOBACCO

It is hard to imagine the sleepy town of Port Tobacco as a major seaport, but before the Revolution it was a Royal Port of Entry. In Charles County, several restored Port Tobacco buildings attest to the town's history.

The Dove

ST. MARY'S COUNTY

It was here that the history of the European settlers in Maryland began, when the English ships of the Calvert family first touched shore in 1634. County history is clearly visible in the many rebuilt and restored buildings that mark the state's earliest days.

In 1634, the first English settlers arrived near the present site of St. Mary's City aboard two tiny vessels, the Ark and the Dove. The reconstructed Dove is docked in the St. Mary's River during spring and summer months.

The Dove

The Dove

THE DOVE

A visit to the Dove gives guests a chilling appreciation for the hardships of the Atlantic crossing in the seventeenth century. Costumed crew members, speaking in a broad cockney accent, explain the ship and the trip to visitors.

35

State House

Godiah Spray

Godiah Spray

Farthing's Ordinary

ST. MARY'S CITY

Maryland's first capital was founded in 1634 at St. Mary's. State government met there until the capital was moved to Annapolis. In 1934, to commemorate the 300th anniversary of the landing of the first settlers from England, a reconstuction of the orginal State House was completed in St. Mary's City. Nearby archaeological digs mark other important early sites. "Dyett and Drinke" in Farthing's Ordinary, one of Maryland's earliest taverns. The plantation of Godiah Spray is recreated in St. Mary's City. It is typical of seventeenth century farms.

SOTTERLEY MANSION

Sotterley, dating from 1777, faces the Patuxent River near Hollywood. Extensive English gardens surround the mansion.

Amish farmers, St. Mary's County

Point Lookout State Park

POINT LOOKOUT STATE PARK

Point Lookout State Park, in St. Mary's County, contains the remains of a Civil War prison. A monument nearby honors the Confederate soldiers who died while imprisoned there.

Crisfield in Somerset County

THE EASTERN SHORE

They begin to pop up not long after your car touches down on the eastern side of the Chesapeake Bay Bridge: those bumper stickers that read "IS THERE LIFE WEST OF THE CHESAPEAKE BAY?" Ask any Eastern Shoreman and the answer will be a resounding "No!".

Those who live on the flat farmlands east of the Bay are more likely to think of themselves first as residents of the Shore and second as Marylanders. You'll note, by the way, that "Eastern Shore" is properly capitalized (as opposed to western shore). There is an old joke about the woman who died at age 83 in some Eastern Shore hamlet. Her parents had brought her there from Baltimore when she was still in diapers. "She was OK", commented one of her neighbors at graveside, "for a foreigner".

On several occasions there has even been serious talk about the Shore seceding from the state of Maryland. But it hasn't kept our neighbors to the east from welcoming guests to their land of sunshine and water with open arms and big platters of steamed crabs and fried chicken.

But there's a lot more to the place than the beach at Ocean City and fresh seafood. Sadly, most visitors miss the real Eastern Shore as they speed from points west along Route 50 hell-bent for the ocean. Three or four blocks off the macadam strip, a slower-paced life goes on oblivious to the mayhem. This is the Eastern Shore that its residents cherish.

Nine counties in all share the Maryland portion of the Delmarva Peninsula. There are three distinct regions, each with a unique character. The lower Shore is a summer vacation mecca for hundreds of thousands of sun-worshipers. The middle Shore, with towns like Oxford, Easton, and St. Michaels, captures the historical and cultural limelight. From the Bay Bridge north to the Mason-Dixon line, the upper Shore is an area of placid farmlands.

The counties of Dorchester, Wicomico, Worcester, and Somerset, are as far to the southeast as one can go in Maryland. Salisbury, the county seat of Wicomico County, is the business and transportation center of the lower Shore. Salisbury sits in the middle of chicken country. Hundreds of signs in front of family farms up and down the landscape announce that the farmer raises chickens for Perdue, Cookin' Good, or Country Pride processors.

In addition, there are firms that make business forms, heavy equipment, and gasoline pumps. The Salisbury Wicomico Airport is the largest, best-equipped facility on the Eastern Shore and there is direct rail service by ConRail.

There is culture as well. Salisbury State College houses the Wildfowl Museum, a celebration of the Shore's famous local art form. The Salisbury Zoo is recognized as one of the nation's finest small zoos, in a beautiful riverside setting.

Cambridge, the focal point of Dorchester County, is a short hop up Route 50. The landscape here is much the same as elsewhere on the Shore. Chicken farms and sprawling corn fields sit side-by-side. Most Dorchester Countians make their livings not on the land, however, but in one of the county's many industrial firms. Factories in Dorchester County turn out electronic gear, frozen food, processed seafood, printed material, and industrial wire products.

Near Cambridge is the Blackwater National Wildlife Refuge. During the fall and winter, the fields and salt marshes here are literally covered with tens of thousands of geese who winter in the refuge. A sizable population of Bald Eagles also calls Blackwater home.

To the south are Worcester and Somerset Counties. Worcester occupies all of Maryland's Atlantic shoreline. Ocean City, perched along a narrow barrier island at the eastern end of Route 50, is the vacation capital of the state. Ask nearly any Baltimorean where he or she will go for vacation. In their peculiar dialect they will reply "Downyashun"—down the ocean. They don't mean Atlantic City or Wildwood, either.

There are miles of white, sandy beaches on one side of Ocean City and a shallow, placid Assawoman Bay on the other. Most come here for the sun and sand, but plenty head for the piers after the marlin, tuna, and bluefish that live in the offshore Atlantic or the flounder in the bay. When the sun goes down hundreds of restaurants and clubs open their doors to greet the sunburned vacationers. Shops sell everything from bathing attire to imports from the Orient.

Assateague Island attracts many campers and nature-lovers. A twenty-minute drive from Ocean City, the State and National Seashore Parks here offer a diverse and interesting series of half-day classes on fishing, clamming, birding, beach-walking, and dozens of other quiet, natural pursuits.

The glitter falls away quickly outside Ocean City and the rural character returns. Driving south along Route 113 from Salisbury, one passes through a number of small, farm-based Eastern Shore towns. The first is Snow Hill, county seat of Worcester. Chartered in 1686, Snow Hill's streets are lined with ancient houses, many with tall cupolas for ship-watching. All Hallows Episcopal Church, with its 200-year old cemetery, is the town's historic centerpiece. Nearby, there are several fine state parks: Shad Landing, Milburn Landing, all along the deep, black waters of the Pocomoke River.

Princess Anne, in Somerset County, also mirrors lower Eastern Shore history. The village's pride is the Teackle Mansion, an 18th century plantation-style home built by one of the Shore's leading early statesmen. Other historic homes are open in October, during old Princess Anne Days. The University of Maryland Eastern Shore anchors one end of Main Street.

Crisfield, locally called "The Seafood Capital of the World", is about as far south on the Shore as one can go and still be in Maryland. The narrow alleys are piled on either side with oyster shells, barrels, and the ephemera of water life. Boats leave here for Smith Island, a small flat speck on the Chesapeake Bay where the soft crab population exceeds humans by about a thousand-to-one.

Ocean City

The middle Shore, flat and watery, looks much like the rest of Maryland's east. Just look carefully, however, and its distinct personality is apparent. This is real Eastern Shore class—a bit snobbish, perhaps, but with a lot of hospitality just under the surface. Easton, in Talbot County, is the unofficial regional capital. But two blocks (and a century or so) off Route 50, the best of the past is preserved here, pleasantly blended with the present. The quiet streets are lined with historic structures whose shop windows feature decoys, casual clothes, Eastern Shore art, and antiques. An hour or two at a table at the Tidewater Inn gives the visitor a real appreciation of the middle Shore.

Oxford and St. Michaels are nearby. The town names are seldom mentioned separately, perhaps because of the Tred Avon Ferry that links them. The ferry has run longer than any other in the country, carrying millions of cars and passengers across the river of the same name. Each village has a small museum, and many shops with Eastern Shore merchandise. St. Michaels is a major yachting center, and races in Chesapeake Bay log canoes are run on the river here all summer. The traditional craft carry an enormous amount of sail, and the crew must hang dizzyingly over the side to keep their canoes upright.

Caroline County is a bit more rural. Manufacturing here accounts for all but a small portion of the employment, and much of that is dependent on the farm. The County Seat is at Denton, and nearby are Tuckahoe and Martinak State Parks. The fishing is great, and many visitors come here to try their luck in the small lakes and ponds. When the summer tourists have left the signs go up advertising hunting trips, guide services, and wildfowl dressing.

Centerville is the seat of Queen Anne's County, a farm and food-processing center. This charming Eastern Shore town centers around a courthouse that has been the scene of legal wrangling since 1792. Look for Lawyer's Row, a collection of tiny restored colonial homes that still houses law offices. Centreville embodies the quiet, unassuming style of the middle Shore.

There's a burgeoning economy in the middle Shore, hidden perhaps by the white sails of the waterfront and behind the restored facades of the small towns. Much manufacturing is land or water related. Many residents work in seafood packing plants and canneries, though the days of huge truck farms growing thousands of tons of produce are gone. Nestled among the cornfields are firms which make plastics, electrical equipment, trailers, marine gear, and power tools. Companies like the steady, reliable work force. After all, with miles of peaceful rivers, quiet solitude, great fishing and hunting, and a generally good standard of living, who would ever want to leave?

Kent and Cecil Counties make up the upper Eastern Shore. Both have the Chesapeake Bay to the west and Delaware to the east, and both are predominantly farmland. The Bay and the rivers here offer excellent fishing, hunting, and boating. But to most tourists, the upper Shore is virtually unknown.

Chestertown is one of the Shore's loveliest towns. Home of Washington College, it is known for its many Revolutionary War homes along the Chester River waterfront. The first president granted the use of his name for the college, and served on its Board of Governors, and that institution is still the town's heartbeat.

The economy, however, is something different. Chestertown, and other upper Shore burgs, almost seem to be encroaching on what would otherwise be valuable farmland. Over half of the upper Shore relies on farming for its living, and many of the non-farmers turn to the Chesapeake Bay for a livelihood. Workboats can still be seen at Rock Hall, which has been a fishing center for three hundred years, and at Dominion on Kent Island.

Cecil County hugs Maryland's northeast corner, and is an important corridor for Baltimore-Wilmington-Philadelphia and north. The seat, Elkton, is an industrial town. Plants here manufacture chemicals, industrial products, medical wares, textiles, and rocket motors. No doubt the fact that Routes 40 and 95, the East Coast's most heavily-travelled commercial routes, run through the heart of the county contribute to the county's industrial success.

In character Cecil County is as much like the Maryland heartland as the Eastern Shore. Farming is not as widespread, though for recreation its residents still look to the Chesapeake Bay and the Susquehanna River. The Susquehanna flats offer excellent fishing and provide some of the best waterfowl hunting on the eastern seaboard. Elk Neck State Forest, Elk Neck State Park, and Susquehanna State Park host thousands of campers each season.

There's always a great temptation to stay here, to become a waterman, or just to settle comfortably into the Eastern Shore life. Many Marylanders choose to retire to the Shore, and many notable Washington figures maintain lavish summer homes here. Yet most things go along at the same pace as they have for centuries. New ideas are accepted when there is some benefit to the Shore's natives, but never at the expense of radically changing the landscape or the special Eastern Shore personality. Happily, it's always nearby—just a quick hop across the Bay Bridge.

Ocean City

WORCESTER COUNTY

Maryland's Eastern Shore playground – that is how most state residents know Worcester County. The beach is what draws people to the state's only county on the edge of Atlantic, but there is much more here. A sense of history dictates much in the small farm towns, and a close link to nature still controls life here. A host of luxurious highrise hotels and condominiums dot the beach in Ocean City, Maryland's only seaside resort. Referred to by its many fans as "OC", the ocean playground opens its doors to nearly a million visitors each year.

Ocean City

Ocean City

Ocean City

Ocean City

Ocean City

OCEAN CITY

Ocean City is a pleasure mecca. During the day the white sand along miles of beaches attracts surfers and beachcombers. At night, the town's restaurants, clubs, and boardwalk attractions are filled with newly-tan visitors.

Ocean City

OCEAN CITY
Any bright summer day finds the beaches at Ocean City packed with sun-worshippers. When the sun goes down the action moves to "the boards"—Ocean City's boardwalk. Many find thrills on the dozens of exciting rides, or nostalgia on the old merry-go-round.

Ocean City

OCEAN CITY

While the beach is the main attraction in "OC", plenty of vacationers come for the fishing, sailing, and other water sports. Deep sea fishing parties leave from the old-town Ocean City docks daily for bluefish, tuna, and the sleek white marlin.

Snow Hill

SNOW HILL
The county seat of Worcester County, Snow Hill is filled with three centuries of fine old homes.

WICOMICO COUNTY

Salisbury, the Wicomico County seat, is the center of economic activity on the Eastern Shore. It is home to the shore's largest industries, as well as Salisbury State College.

Wicomico River

Newtown, Salisbury

Poplar Hill

Pemberton Hall

POPLAR HILL

Poplar Hill, a Federal mansion in Salisbury dating from 1820 is one of the finest early homes on the shore. Colonial Williamsburg copied much of its woodwork as part of their own restoration efforts.

NEWTOWN

The Newtown Historic District, which surrounds Poplar Hill in Salisbury, is a collection of pristinely-restored Victorian homes that were built after two disastrous fires swept the neighborhood in 1860 and 1886.

PEMBERTON HALL

Pemberton Hall is the 1805 home of Salisbury's founder, Colonel Isaac Handy. It will be the centerpiece of an historic park.

Deale Island, Somerset County

SOMERSET COUNTY

If any single county in Maryland can be called the seafood capital, it would have to be Somerset.
A fleet of wooden skipjacks still dredges the bay waters here for oysters, and watermen set out for crabs
and fin fish as well. A typical Somerset County lanscape? Look for piles of crab pots and oyster shells
near a white clapboarded farmhouse.

Crisfield

CRISFIELD

Workboats call at the seafood packers and processors in Crisfield to unload the daily catch. Most are from the offshore islands of Smith and Tangier.

Spocott Windmill

DORCHESTER COUNTY

A typical Dorchester County landscape would present miles and miles of flat farmland filled with corn or soybeans. But there is more here than farmers and watermen. One of the state's preeminent waterfowl sanctuaries and home to a growing flock of Bald Eagles, Blackwater, is near Cambridge. History pokes its way into the twentieth century here too. Just take a walk through Cambridge, East New Market, or many other Dorchester towns to see the past and present merge.

SPOCOTT WINDMILL, DORCHESTER COUNTY

Spocott Windmill, at Lloyds in Dorchester County, is a 1791 reconstruction of an earlier mill. It once ground meal from dozens of county farms.

Cambridge

HIGH STREET, CAMBRIDGE

Cambridge's historic High Street is a wealth of well-preserved buildings representing 200 years of small-town Eastern Shore architecture.

Tred Avon River, Talbot County

TALBOT COUNTY

It is hard to imagine that many Talbot County towns were once ports of entry, but the county was a major center of trade in its early history. Today, many come here for fishing and hunting, and many choose to retire here, where "The Land of Pleasant Living" is best personified.

Hooper's Strait Lighthouse

HOOPER'S STRAIGHT LIGHTOUSE

Once the sentinel for bay navigators, the Hooper's Strait Lighthouse has a new home at the Chesapeake Bay Maritime Museum in St. Michael's.

LOG CANOE RACES

Log canoe races are the highlight of the sailing season in St. Michael's and Oxford. The wooden boats, with their huge sails, are traditional Eastern Shore craft.

Easton

St. Michael's

Chesapeake Bay Maritime Museum, St. Michael's

Sunrise, Kent Island

QUEEN ANNE'S COUNTY

When the Chesapeake Bay Bridge touches down on the Eastern Shore it is Queen Anne's County that greets those bound for vacation. It is more than just a highway to the beach, however. Queen Anne's looks to the Bay for much of its livelihood. Watermen sail daily from Kent and Tilghman Islands in search of oysters, crabs, and fish.

Wye Oak

Kent Island

The Chesapeake Bay Bridge

Queen Anne's County

THE CHESAPEAKE BAY BRIDGE

The Chesapeake Bay Bridge is the motorists' gateway to the Eastern Shore.

Wye Oak

Maryland's official State Tree, the Wye Oak is estimated to be well over 400 years old. Its gnarled trunk is over 21 feet in circumference.

CAROLINE COUNTY

Farmland marks the character of Caroline County. Farmers here growing primarily grain and vegetable crops. For recreation, Caroline Countians turn to the water. There is excellent fishing and boating at any of several state parks.

DENTON

Denton is the Caroline County seat. Its courthouse shares space on the Green with Victorian homes and law offices.

Martinak State Park

MARTINAK STATE PARK

Near Denton, Martinak State Park has 99 acres of campgrounds, fishing, boating, and hunting along the Choptank river.

Kent County

KENT COUNTY

Sportsmen and naturalists count Kent County as one of their Maryland favorites. There are abundant waterfowl management areas as well as hunting and fishing. The county seat, Chestertown, is also the upper shore's commercial center.

Chestertown

Famous for its fine old riverfront houses, Chestertown is also home to Washington College, one of the Shore's oldest and most respected institutions. Little has changed here—on the surface—for two centuries.

Chesapeake and Delaware Canal

CECIL COUNTY

Since 1608, when Captain John Smith arrived in what would become Cecil County, the Chesapeake Bay and Elk River have played important roles in the county's development. Sportsmen flock here year-round for fishing, hunting, and camping. Since World War II, the county has also become one of the state's most important industrial centers.

CHESAPEAKE AND DELAWARE CANAL

Chesapeake City is astride the Chesapeake and Delaware Canal, which connects the Chesapeake and the Delaware Bays. A modern canal, the C&D is heavily traveled by both pleasure and commercial craft.

Elk Neck State Park

ELK NECK STATE PARK

Elk Neck State Park provides acres of camping facilities, boating, and fishing at the head of the Elk River near Elkton.

Deer Creek, Harford County

CENTRAL MARYLAND

Not far from the western beaches of the Chesapeake Bay the landscape begins to change. The land begins to undulate, gently-rolling hills sheltering a clapboarded house and large barn in one valley, a sprawling aerospace facility in another. From the air all roads lead to two cities: Baltimore, on the banks of the Patapsco River, and the seat of national power a bit to the south, Washington, D.C.

Five counties and Baltimore City make up this region often called "the Corridor Counties" by state economic experts. The name comes from the fact that several important highways, notably US Route 95, slice through Maryland here on their relentless path from Boston to Washington. Baltimore anchors central Maryland, and thirty-five miles down the road the nation's capital, though not a political part of the state, is Maryland's second most important center of influence.

But "Corridor Counties"—a name that emphasizes asphalt paths through the state's most productive economic area belittles the role that region plays in Maryland's history and modern development. Central Maryland is indeed the heartland of the state in more ways than one. If there is a Maryland breadbasket, this is it. It is also the commercial, cultural, and social hub around which the rest of Maryland revolves (though many in Salisbury, Leonardtown, or Cumberland would loathe to admit it).

Time was many people thought Baltimore City was nothing more than a sooty smudge on the landscape somewhere between Washington and Philadelphia. Adjectives frequently applied to the city on the banks of the Patapsco included "backwater" and "provincial".

Should any of those detractors leave the mayhem of Route 95 and head for downtown Baltimore now they would discover a thriving, modern, and beautiful waterfront town. The Baltimore Renaissance began in the mid-1970's, and has left Baltimore with a sparkling new Inner Harbor focused on the Harborplace development and a convention center that is booked years in advance. There's a harborfront outdoor concert hall, the award-winning National Aquarium, and dozens of new hotels and restaurants.

Baltimore City has made the cover of Time magazine and has been the spotlight in every important travel publication since its rebirth. Mayors from other older cities have flocked to Baltimore looking for solutions to their own problems. All this hoopla has not been without economic repercussions. As Baltimore loses manufacturing jobs demand for workers in service businesses helps take up the slack.

So Baltimore is a success story, a new and dramatically-changed city. Thankfully, however, under the facade of a scintillating tourist town Baltimore is still the same. Its citizens still look to the harbor for an economic base and still look to their small inner city neighborhoods for family living. Many Italian Baltimoreans still live near the corner of Pratt and Albermarle Streets and Greek town is still on Eastern Avenue. Everyone still roots for the Baltimore Orioles.

In 1729, the state legislature passed a resolution creating a market town around what is now the Inner Harbor. By then, Fells Point and Jones Town to the east had long been prosperous port towns. It wasn't long, however, before Baltimore eclipsed the earlier settlements, and by 1760 all three had merged into Baltimore Town.

The first shipment of wheat from Baltimore was made in 1758, and within a year or two dozens of flour mills dotted the Jones Falls, Gwynns Falls, and other streams that fell from the hills of Baltimore County to the Baltimore harbor. It was wheat that built Baltimore trade, and along with the growth in trade came a boom in other maritime industries: shipbuilding, ship chandlering, and of course a powerful merchant class.

Baltimore's port is still the nation's third largest. The old offices along Water Street and Redwood Street—just a block from Harborplace—are still home to shipping companies and customs agents. Instead of wheat, holds in the harbor are filled with coal, cement, and automobiles. Baltimore is a transportation hub, linking the port with every major population center via rail and road. An established network of manufacturers and financial service firms have grown around the harbor to support, and often supplant, the city's mercantile interests.

Baltimore's factories are known the world over: General Motors, Lever Brothers, McCormick Spices among others. The city is the financial pulse of the entire state. Five major trust companies are headquartered here in a cluster of highrises blocks from the waterfront. Insurance also plays an important role in Maryland's economy, and Baltimore is home to two nationally-respected casualty companies and a host of smaller surety firms.

Though there is a long tradition of economic strength here, largely supported by mercantile interests, Baltimore has not come this far without the same growing pains as other East Coast cities. Manufacturing jobs began to evaporate in the 1960's. For every large manufacturer still here, another has either closed their local operations or severely curtailed its production. This has meant severe adjustments. As manufacturing jobs disappear the new tourist industry has grown. But the loss of high-wage "Rust Belt" jobs is not easily balanced by lower-paying service employment. Visiting tourists and conventioneers mean millions of new dollars in the local economy, yet the Baltimore business scene is still in the midst of the most far-reaching changes since the Industrial Revolution.

Change has filtered from the boardrooms to the city's neighborhoods as the focus of its citizens broadens. Baltimore looks increasingly to its past, and the city has been swept with an almost manic effort to preserve its old homes and landmarks. The result is visible in dozens of newly-proud residential enclaves: Fells Point, Reservoir Hill, Seton Hill, Union Square, and Bolton Hill among others. Baltimore has been a pioneer in urban development programs that encourage individual homeowners to restore their fine old homes. The neighborhood pride has always been there, but of late it has received enthusiastic support from City Hall under the aegis of Mayor William Donald Schaefer, the city's most vociferous booster.

The Baltimore Symphony Orchestra calls the stunning Joseph Meyerhoff Concert Hall home, and the nearby Lyric Theatre hosts opera, ballet, and Broadway shows. Morris Mechanic Theatre, a short walk from the water, stages Broadway productions.

The Inner Harbor in Baltimore City

Center Stage is widely-respected for its repertory presentations of established theatre and its bold tradition of staging plays by new playwrights. Peabody Conservatory is the musical heart of Maryland, located on Mount Vernon Place just north of the Inner Harbor.

Near Johns Hopkins University, the Baltimore Museum of Art houses several impressive collections, including the famous Cone Collection of Modern Art. The Walters Art Gallery has a century-long tradition of fine presentations of classic works of European and Asian art, and a host of small private galleries have sprung up in recent years to display the works of up-and-coming artists.

In the summer months, Memorial Stadium comes to life as the home of the Baltimore Orioles who boast the "winningest" tradition in professional baseball. The Baltimore Skipjacks play host to the American Hockey League Teams on the ice in the Civic Center, and the Baltimore Blast has a fine winning record in professional indoor soccer.

For over a century the people of Baltimore have welcomed visitors; first the immigrants who stepped on these shores for the first time at Locust Point, and now the tourists who flock to the city for its myriad attractions. Everyone heads first for Harborplace, two shining pavilions on the harbor basin that house dozens of shops and fine eateries. Harborplace has, since its opening in 1976, become the focus for all Inner Harbor activities. The harbor taxies that ply the water, stop at the National Aquarium and the Science Center just a stone's throw away. Guests interested in history take in the ramparts at Fort McHenry and visit the B&O Railroad Museum, The Peale Museum, Maryland Historical Society, and many smaller historic collections.

Oliver Wendell Holmes called Baltimore a "culinary capital", referring to the bounty from the shores of the Chesapeake Bay. Restaurants still feature oysters (only in the "R" months, of course), steamed crabs, Maryland Fried Chicken, and other specialties in a fine southern tradition. As the tourist industry has grown, restaurants have appeared on the Baltimore scene to satisfy any palate—from Szechuan to steamed mussels.

It is a city in the midst of unrelenting change. Baltimoreans have responded to the economic upheaval and are working to carve a solid path into the twenty-first century.

Baltimore's influence spreads way beyond its boundaries. The Baltimore metropolitan area consists of the counties of Baltimore, Harford, Carroll, Howard, and much of Anne Arundel in southern Maryland. While the population of the city itself has declined over the past three decades, its importance as a center for employment has not. By eight o'clock in the morning in any of these surrounding counties the roads will be clogged with commuters making the daily trek to Baltimore. The jobs are still here, only drawing workers from a wider and wider area.

Baltimore County surrounds the city on the east, north, and west. The two are politically separate, but their pasts and their futures are permanently bound. The city provides an outlet for the manufacturing firms that fill county industrial parks, and the farms of the county's rolling hills raise the fresh produce that fills the shelves of Baltimore City markets.

Among the county's first settlers was an English immigrant, George Alsop. After arriving at the end of a torturous five-month Atlantic crossing, he wrote "There is no place on earth that can parallel this fertile and pleasant piece of ground." Baltimore County remains an inviting landscape, with its gently-rolling hills and pleasant climate. But under its rural facade, the county has changed much since Mr. Alsop first set foot here. Diversity is the byword today, for the county offers opportunity in everything from truck farming to missile launching systems, dairying to computer technology.

Much is controlled from just a few buildings surrounding the courthouse green in Towson, the county seat. Once a sleepy farming community, Towson has boomed since the Second World War. Today many of the old two-story stone houses have been replaced by steel-and-glass towers and the town is a bustling retail, legal and financial center. Nestled among the modern highrises are dozens of proud Victorian gingerbread houses, now mostly offices for lawyers and insurance agencies. Countians still come to the original 1855 courthouse for marriage licenses or to trace their property deeds.

During the last two decades, the area just north of Towson has attracted light industry and distribution. Heavy industry is located in the eastern part of the county. Baltimore County firms send products to all corners of the globe with brand names that are widely recognized: Black and Decker power tools, Noxzema, Sweetheart cups, Bendix electronics, and McCormick spices.

There is a long tradition of leisure in Baltimore County apart from its industrial parks. The Maryland Hunt Cup, held every spring, is the annual highlight of the Maryland equestrian season. Jousting, the official state sport, is popular. Meets are sponsored by volunteer firehouses, churches, and equestrian clubs all summer. In Timonium, the midways of the fairgrounds are filled with barkers and games of chance, the barns with prize hogs and sheep, and the arenas with jams and jellies, quilts and handcrafts at the Maryland State Fair in September.

To the east of Baltimore County, the old Philadelphia Road cuts a path through Harford County. Once a stage coach route, colonial taverns and inns dotted this highway that now is lined with gas stations and fast food restaurants. Harford County poked along for decades virtually ignoring the buzz of traffic that sped through on its way elsewhere. But in the 1960's the quiet, rolling hills were discovered by developers and those seeking a peaceful family life. Today, rush hour traffic in the county seat, Bel Air, rivals that along Chesapeake Avenue in Towson.

Harford's farms are declining in number as farmers sell their acreage to developers. But the region has experienced welcome industrial growth, for it has a propitious location along the nation's busiest East Coast throughway. Harford County firms turn out shoes and rainwear for consumers while chemical companies and foundries serve the industrial community.

Harford's northern farmlands are an extension of the horse country of Baltimore County, and as such have been a retreat for the wealthy for many years. At the Ladew Topiary Gardens, the collection of paintings, antiques, and objets d'art in Pleasant Valley House exemplify the lifestyles of the foxhunting set. When the weather is nice it is easy to spot young equestrians practicing jousting or jumping their horses on the wide, rolling fields.

The Chesapeake Bay also plays a major role in Harford County life though not even Marylanders associate the Bay with this northern county. Much of the shoreline is occupied by the Edgewood Arsenal and the Aberdeen Proving Grounds, two military installations that employ thousands of countians. There is little commercial fishing here, and marinas are home to leisure craft rather than workboats. Sports fishing in the Bay and the Susquehanna River are popular Harford County activities. Havre de Grace hosts a Hydroplane Regatta and a Waterfowl Festival every year.

Sam Kirkendall, jousting National Champion, demonstrates ring jousting, Harford County.

As farms became residential communities and industry absorbed the lost agricultural jobs, Harford Countians began an effort to save some of their past. Small museums testify to the rigor of early farm life. Throughout the summer, early arts and crafts are demonstrated at the Steppingstone Museum in Susquehanna State Park. In Bel Air, the Hays House is operated as a museum of Harford County memorabilia and Rock Run Mill in Susquehanna State Park still stone-grinds meal as it has since 1794. Reminders of the county's heritage help to put its rapid growth into perspective.

Howard County, due west of Baltimore City, has gone through many of the same growing pains as Harford. Not long ago the income of nearly every resident was somehow linked to the soil. Those that didn't grow produce or raise dairy cattle either worked the dozens of water-powered grist mills that lined the banks of Howard County's streams and rivers or transported the farm goods to the city.

While life in the county seat, Ellicott City, was moving at a rural pace, the Baltimore suburbs were splitting their seams. It was inevitable that new communities spring up, since the county is close to both Baltimore and Washington. The "new town" of Columbia, on Route 29 convenient to both cities, welcomed its first residents in 1967.

Columbia was carved out of Howard County farms, founded on the premise that a city can be efficient and comfortable for both living and working. Nearly a hundred thousand Howard Countians call Columbia home and half the businesses in the county are located here. Columbia has attracted firms whose names are known around the globe: General Electric and Bendix Aerospace, for instance. It is difficult to deny the success of the idea that spawned Columbia. There's a children's zoo and an outdoor concert hall, and the diverse housing pockets are separated by parks, lakes, and convenient shopping areas.

Perhaps it was nearby Columbia that spared Ellicott City from rampant development. The steep Main Street winds between stone houses and shops as it has since the late 1700's. Howard County courts and offices are perched on a hill overlooking the old town center, close enough to be convenient yet distant enough to be inconspicuous. The town was once one of the state's busiest milling and manufacturing centers. Now the ancient stone buildings are home to antique shops and art galleries, anchored by the Baltimore and Ohio Railroad Museum along the banks of the Patapsco.

The focus begins to change as the distance from Baltimore increases to the southwest. Somewhere along Route 95, perhaps near Laurel or Greenbelt, the people begin to think of themselves more as Washingtonians than as Marylanders. "Baltimore" is a curious place to visit on weekends, but not to be taken seriously as a city of any influence.

Montgomery County is north of the nation's capital, and because of its proximity to the seemingly-endless job pool that is the federal government, it is Maryland's most affluent county.

President James Madison fled to Montgomery County when Washington was attacked in the War of 1812, and generations of Marylanders still do the same at the close of every business day.

Yesterday the principal economic activity was farming. Today high technology, notably biotechnology and telecommunications, is pursued in industrial parks among the county's rolling hills. Half of the county's employers are engaged in some sort of research and development. The Federal government has spilled across the District of Columbia border. The National Institutes of Health, Naval Medical Center, and National Bureau of Standards are among the federal installations in Montgomery County.

Just a century ago the main thoroughfare through the county was not interstate 70, but instead the Chesapeake and Ohio Canal. Narrow mule drawn canal boats plied it from the Allegheny Mountains to Georgetown, bringing farm products into Washington. The Chesapeake and Ohio Canal Museum in Potomac recalls those days, attracting hundreds of hikers and family picnicers each summer.

But the canal area, and nearby Great Falls, is only a small part of the county's open spaces. There are three large regional parks and countless neighborhood recreational areas. Montgomery County is a mecca for area golfers, with six public courses and 25 private golf clubs. No doubt every summer weekend the legislative discussions move from the Halls of Congress to the putting greens of Montgomery County.

There is much of history here as well. In Rockville, the county seat, the Beall-Dawson House is home to the county historical society. Many small villages still have the rural flavor that characterized the entire county just a generation or so ago.

Prince George's County just east of Washington, shares Montgomery's fortunate location next to the capital. Its industrial parks are also filled with firms engaged in all types of research in computer technology, satellite systems, and electronics. But Prince George's is almost two different worlds, for to the south the landscape is like that of the tobacco country of southern Maryland while the areas closer to Washington are enclaves of modern development.

County history begins not long after the first English settlements were carved out of the forest. It was a part of the vital north-south trading corridor during the 1700's. Tobacco was King, and in southern Prince George's it still is. By the time the commuters have arrived at the New Carrollton subway station on their way to work the chant of the tobacco auctioneer in Upper Marlboro has filled the sales barns for hours.

Prince George's is justly proud of its role in Maryland's past. The county's story is told in the pictures, photographs, and collections of the Indian Queen Tavern, a museum (where, of course, George Washington slept) in Bladensburg. Adelphi Mill, in the town of the same name, ground grain in the early 1800's and is now restored and used as a community center. Maryland's greatest concentration of historic churches is here as well. St. Thomas's, in Croom, dates from 1732 and is but one of half-a-dozen eighteenth century houses of worship that still welcome guests.

Respect for the past has not kept Prince George's County from moving energetically into the twentieth century. The oldest airport in the United States was established at College Park in 1909 and was the beginning of the county's love of flight. Andrews Air Force Base in Camp Springs is the home of Air Force One. The Goddard Space Flight Center is the hub of all NASA tracking activities as well as the development ground for several generations of space vehicles.

Nearby University of Maryland, in College Park, grew from a small agricultural college to a major educational institution. It is still known for the excellence of its agricultural program, and many of its graduates have moved from the campus just a few miles north to the U.S. Department of Agriculture's Research Center in Beltsville. Farming obviously is still close to the surface here.

Surely Prince George's is among the most economically diverse of Maryland's subdivisions, yet in its diversity it mirrors much of Maryland's heartland. There are industrial parks where farms once covered the landscape, but as Captain John Smith wrote of central Maryland in 1608, "Heaven and earth seemed never to have agreed better to frame a place for man's commodious and delightful habitation." The same can easily be said today.

HARFORD COUNTY

"Yesterday Reflected in Today" is the title of a Harford County travel brochure, and the slogan aptly describes the county's attitude toward its rich historical assets. The county seat, Bel Air, has managed to retain a nineteenth century facade, but under the surface a modern political and business center thrives.

LIRIODENDRON MANSION

Built in 1898, Liriodendron Mansion is today a center for Harford County history and cultural arts. The "Gatsbyesque" house was the summer home of Dr. Howard A. Kelly, whose early success in the treatment of cancer helped make Johns Hopkins Hospital a world-renowned institution.

Farmland, Harford County

Ladew Topiary Gardens

LADEW TOPIARY GARDENS

The Ladew Topiary Gardens, near Jarrettsville in Harford County, are known throughout the gardening world for their extraordinary carved topiary plants. Pleasant Valley, the home of the gardens' creator, Mr. Harvey Ladew, contains a fine collection of objets d'art and foxhunting memorabilia.

Harford County

Madison R. Mitchell

Concord Point Lighthouse

Jousting is the Maryland State Sport. Harford County

HAVRE DE GRACE

Concord Point Light is the oldest continuously-used lighthouse on the East Coast. The light played an important role in shoreline protection during the War of 1812, when British troops ascended the Chesapeake as far as Havre de Grace.

DECOY CARVING

Madison R. Mitchell, of Havre de Grace, is a nationally-known waterfowl carver. A decoy carving competion is held each year in this town along the Susquehanna River.

Baltimore County landscape, just minutes from downtown Baltimore

BALTIMORE COUNTY

   Though Baltimore County surrounds the city of the same name on three sides, most of the county's landscape is rural. Towson, the county seat, has changed from a quiet village to a burgeoning legal, financial, and retail center, yet as one travels north to Pennsylvania, highrise offices and industrial parks gradually give way to rolling farmland.

Towson

TOWSON

The county seat of Baltimore County, Towson, had humble beginnings prior to the Revolution. Today, the area is a bustling legal, retail, and financial center with modern buildings providing a sharp contrast to the Victorian homes that remain.

THE HUNT CUP

Baltimore County's Greenspring Valley hosts the Maryland Hunt Cup each May, the highlight of the Maryland equestrian season. Thousands of visitors picnic from their tailgates or in the rolling fields to watch the competition.

Monkton

Hampton Mansion

Hunt Valley

HUNT VALLEY

The Hunt Valley Mall is a modern shopping complex north of Towson, in one of the fastest growing light-industrial sections of Maryland.

HAMPTON MANSION

North of Towson, the Hampton National Historic Site is a magnificent late-Georgian plantation house built by one of Baltimore County's wealthiest families, the Ridgelys. It contains a fine collection of Federal and Empire furnishings.

Tall ships visit Baltimore's Inner Harbor, July, 1986

BALTIMORE CITY

The financial and cultural focal point of the entire state, Baltimore has a fortunate location astride the Patapsco River. The City has been an important port of entry for over two centuries, and in recent years part of its working harbor has been transformed into a dazzling tourist center. Baltimore's ethnic neighborhoods and its reputation for hospitality, coupled with a careful plan for moving successfully into the Twenty First Century have made the city one of America's most dynamic urban centers.

Fort McHenry

FORT McHENRY

"By the dawn's early light", on September 14, 1814, Francis Scott Key searched the horizon for the Stars and Stripes, flying over Baltimore's Fort McHenry. The first fortifications were built in 1776, and the fort served the military for over a century and a half.

Baltimore City

BALTIMORE CITY

Baltimore's financial center glistens like a string of jewels after dark. Once an area of broken-down warehouses and rotting piers, the harbor is now a magnet for tourists and businesses alike.

MOUNT VERNON PLACE

With the striking Washington Monument as its centerpiece, Mount Vernon is one of Baltimore's most pristine historic neighborhoods. There are many more downtown residential sections undergoing restoration or redevelopment in this city that takes pride in its fine neighborhoods and dedicated residents.

BALTIMORE CITY HALL

Rather than raze the 1867 Baltimore City Hall, in 1975 the city fathers wisely chose to restore its facade, keeping many of its most impressive interior features as well. City Hall has a magnificent 110-foot rotunda, capped with a gold gilt cupola.

Columbia

HOWARD COUNTY

Few of Maryland's counties display the rich diversity of Howard County. Columbia, along a major corridor from Baltimore to Washington, is a modern, well-planned "new town" that combines comfortable residential life with an environment that fosters economic development. Yet the county still has the best of rural living as well, its rolling hills dotted with prosperous farms, exquisite estates, and friendly villages.

COLUMBIA

A project of respected developer James Rouse, Columbia was one of the nation's first fully-planned cities. Its neighborhoods and business centers are conveniently located, the entire town focused on Columbia Mall.

Ellicott City

ELLICOTT CITY

Three Quaker Brothers, Joseph, John, and Andrew Ellicott, built iron and grist mills along the Patapsco River in what is now Ellicott City. Today, antique shops, art galleries, and restaurants line old Main Street.

Montpelier Mansion

PRINCE GEORGE'S COUNTY

The auctioneer's voice sings out in Prince George's County tobacco warehouses in March and April. Many of the county's towns - Bowie, Upper Marlboro, Oxon Hill - go along as though nearby Washington was still the small swampy town it was 250 years ago. But the influence of the nation's capital in Prince George's is undeniable, as federal facilities have spilled across the District of Columbia border.

MONTPELIER MANSION

Montpilier Mansion was most likely built by Mayor Thomas Snowden between 1770 and 1785. Besides its fine architecture it is significant because of its famous guests which included George Washington, Abagail Adams and Franklin Roosevelt. Today, besides the mansion and grounds there is also a Cultural Arts Center on the site.

Air Force One

ANDREWS AIR FORCE BASE

"The Gateway to the U.S.", Andrews Air Force Base is the first bit of the nation seen by the many international leaders who land here on their way to Washington. The base is headquarters for the Strategic Air Command and the pulse of much of the country's air defenses.

AIR FORCE ONE

Andrews Air Force Base, near Camp Springs in Prince George's County, is home to Air Force One, the Presidential aircraft.

NASA/GODDARD SPACE FLIGHT CENTER

The NASA complex in Prince George's County is the hub of all NASA tracking activities world wide. The center is also responsible for the development of unmanned sounding rockets for the future NASA space station. All manned space flight communication goes through the center, as will much of the pre-flight planning.

Belair Mansion

BELAIR MANSION

Built for Governor Samuel Ogle in the 1740's, the Belair Mansion was owned from 1898 to 1955 by the Woodwards. The Woodwards, from New York, are a family prominent in American Horse racing. The stables of the mansion housed such famous horses as Nashua.

MONTGOMERY COUNTY

A county that almost defies description, Montgomery is the wealthiest county in America. It couples extensive park and recreational facilities with excellent opportunity for its residents and a business environment that encourages development. Rapid growth characterizes Montgomery County along its border with the nation's capital, while a quiet rural atmosphere rules the rolling farmlands that spread northward from the Washington Beltway.

GARRETT PARK

Garrett Park is the only town in Montgomery County on the National Register of Historic Places.

Bethesda

BETHESDA

Once a small farm town, Bethesda has become a burgeoning technological and corporate center. It is also home to the National Institutes of Health.

Montgomery County farm, near Gaithersburg

Great Falls

Great Falls

Washington, D.C.

White Flint Mall

GREAT FALLS

Great Falls, and the adjoining Chesapeake and Ohio Canal, attracts thousands of sightseers and history buffs. The C&O Canal Museum is the park's focal point. Birdwatching trips, nature programs, and canal walks originate there all year.

WASHINGTON, D.C.

Though not a political part of Maryland, Washington, D.C. has an undeniable effect on the state—economic, political, and cultural. The effect is most obvious in the Maryland counties that surround the capital.

WHITE FLINT MALL

White Flint is a modern enclosed shopping complex near Rockville, in Montgomery County.

Carroll County near Uniontown

96

WESTERN MARYLAND

Some time between Thanksgiving and Christmas the first snow crosses the Allegheny Mountains into Maryland. Two or three inches is all it takes to paralyze Baltimore City - traffic halts, schools are closed, citizens mob the supermarkets to stock up on canned goods. But in the western part of the state the second recreation season is just starting. The ski lodges open, the lakes freeze for ice skaters, and the cold brings out the real pioneer instincts of Western Marylanders.

It's not necessarily the mountains, however, that announce the beginning of western Maryland. There's a hardy independence, a sense that the focus of the people has unconsciously slipped from urban Baltimore and Washington to rural towns and farm villages. To even the casual visitor the difference is obvious an hour or so west of the Baltimore Beltway.

To better understand, compare the county seat of Carroll County, Westminster, with Towson, less than an hour away. Westminster's Main Street still looks much as it has for a century or so. The town thinks nothing of having the Carroll County Farm Museum practically in its center. It's slower here, and perhaps even a bit friendlier. Bustling Towson on the other hand has become a mini-city of pinstriped lawyers and stockbrokers.

There are plenty of physical changes as well. The first line of mountains is visible from Patrick Street in Frederick, but long before then the landscape has begun its ascent. The dark, rich soil of central Maryland gradually changes to a red loam flecked with rocks. Fields are peppered with gray, harrow-busting boulders, some barely visible above the plowed earth. Quite obviously, it is more difficult to wrest a living from a western Maryland farm than from one to the east.

Perhaps it is the hard life of the settlers that made western Marylanders so independent. Civilization was late in arriving. While the rest of Maryland was going to the theatre and serving afternoon tea, western Marylanders were still worried about Indian attacks.

At its best, life in western Maryland meant unending hard work; at it worst, blizzards in May and even June that could wipe out an entire harvest. A special breed of people came here and stuck it out. Modern life is certainly not as threatening or as difficult, but in many ways one must still be a pioneer to make a home in Washington, Allegany, or Garrett County.

Carroll County is a transition area. It is not urban and it is not yet the mountainous area of western Maryland. The countryside changes little as one drives from Reistertown in Baltimore County to the Carroll County seat, Westminster. The farmhouses and roadside produce stands gradually give way to small factories. Growth has come to this farming county only recently and its villages still retain much of their nineteenth-century flavor.

But change does come to the countryside, and some of Carroll County is now a bedroom suburb to Baltimore City. Farms are becoming developments of colonial homes while fewer and fewer Carroll Countians work in agriculture. Products with nationally-known brand names orginate in sprawling factories and warehouses: London Fog rainwear, books from Random House.

Westminster and its surrounding farm towns offer a quiet enclave for those employed in Baltimore. Most of the county's special attractions reflect the farm life of a century or more ago. In Westminster, the Carroll County Farm Museum depicts rural life at the time of the Civil War, and the county courthouse has served in that capacity since 1838. The streets are lined with brick and wooden buildings that are virtually unchanged since the nineteenth century. Westminster has never been "restored" - it just didn't seem necessary.

The same holds true for many other towns in Carroll County. Taneytown, Union Mills, New Windsor, Uniontown all are pristine examples of small-town life a hundred years ago.

It is in Frederick County that the mountains of Western Maryland begin. Sugarloaf Mountain, one of the state's most famous peaks, is a short hop from downtown Frederick. If Frederick is the beginning of something, it is also the end. The influence of Baltimore, and perhaps even more, Washington, is still felt in the foothills here. Beyond Frederick, Washington may as well be on another continent.

The national capital is less than a hour's drive from the county seat. Washingtonians fill the restaurants and antique shops that line Frederick's Main Street every weekend, and many commute from towns like Buckeystown and Urbana to Capital Hill. Camp David, the Presidential retreat, is in Frederick's Catoctin National Park. So even the President makes the county his weekend home-away-from-home.

Those who live and work in Frederick County find a thriving economy and a perfect environment for raising their families. Frederick County is the state's largest dairy producer, and the manufacturing sector provides jobs for a fifth of Frederick's employed. County firms turn out everything from English muffins to communications equipment, pre-fab houses to electronic relays.

The mountains set the tone for leisure activities here. Catoctin National Park has miles of hiking trails through the forests of chestnut, hickory, and black birch. There is camping here as well as at Cunningham Falls State Park with its dramatic waterfalls, boating, swimming, and ice skating in the winter.

Frederick is the historical centerpiece of the county. It was the scene of the nation's first official repudiation of the Stamp Act in 1765 and has been a significant force in state history ever since. Barbara Fritchie, the elderly Frederick Countian who dared fly the Stars and Stripes as Stonewall Jackson's troops marched through the town is immortalized in John Greenleaf Whittier's poem: "Shoot if you must this old gray head, but spare your country's flag."

Other Frederick residents have also left their mark on the national scene: John Hanson was the first American president under the Articles of Confederation, Francis Scott Key wrote the Star-Spangled Banner, and Roger Brooke Taney was one of the country's greatest Supreme Court Chief Justices. The work of Mother Elizabeth Seton, the first native born American to be canonized by the Catholic Church, is memorialized at her home and shrine, and the Grotto of Lourdes near Emmitsburg. The homes, offices, and final resting places of these patriots attract many history buffs.

By the 1730's the mountain passes just west of Frederick had been breached and enterprising settlers were establishing small farms in the valleys of what would become Washington County. Among the first was Jonathan Hager. In 1739, when he built his house, Hager's Fancy, in what is now downtown Hagerstown, the area was still dense wilderness. Washington County served as a staging point for British and American troops during the French and Indian War in the 1750's. War came again in 1862, near Sharpsburg along the banks of Antietam Creek. When that September

Garrett County

17 ended, nearly 24 thousand troops were dead or wounded in the Washington County countryside. One of the state's loveliest counties had become the scene of the bloodiest single-day battle in the Civil War

Though life here was difficult, the pioneers succeeded in carving homes out of the mountain forests despite the hostile Indians and the bitter climate. Farmers developed a burgeoning small grain economy, much different from the tobacco that dominated the tidewater regions. Mills sprung up along Washington County's many creeks and streams.

The growing season is short, the soil rocky and hilly. Although farming is still an important part of the county economy, manufacturing offers more employment opportunity to its natives. Important national firms have factories here, including Londontown Manufacturing (rainwear), Certain-Teed Products (vinyl siding and pipe), Rust-Oleum (paint), and Mack Trucks.

Washington County is a mountain wonderland, with outdoor activities all year long. The Appalachian Trail crosses Maryland here, and there are hiking trails at Fort Frederick in Big Pool and through the Antietam National Battlefield.

History comes to life here as well, leaving an indelible impression of pioneer life on the county's guests. Jonathan Hager's home in Hagerstown depicts life in the county's early days, and Fort Frederick allows visitors to experience the life of a British infantryman 250 years ago. Life on the C&O Canal is the subject at Barron's C&O Canal Museum, and Civil War relics are on display at several county museums. The past is close to the surface in Washington County, a history permanently guided by the rugged yet beautiful landscape.

Allegany County, just to the west of Washington, is one of only two Maryland counties whose names have their roots in Indian lore (the other is Wicomico, on the Eastern Shore). "Beautiful stream" is a rough translation of the county's name from the original Indian dialect. That is certainly what visitors to Allegany County found two hundred years ago and what they still find today: beautiful streams, dense green forests, and breathtaking mountain peaks.

The spectacular rocky gorge that slices through the mountains of Allegany County, The Narrows, is one of the state's best known geographical wonders. This mountain pass set the stage for the county's future. Because of its location at the crossroads serving Baltimore, Washington, and Pittsburgh, Allegany became a transportation center early in its history. Rails, canals, and wagon trains crossed here, and many historic sites have strong transportation roots: The National Road (Route 40); La Vale Toll Gate House, the first toll gate on the National Road; Western Maryland Railroad Station in Cumberland; and the C&O Canal National Historic Park. Allegany County was the gateway to the rich Ohio Valley and beyond to the far West.

It was only natural, therefore, that the region should become a center of manufacturing. It did, and remains so to this day. Companies in Allegany County send tires, rocket fuels, glass, and paper among other products across the nation. The county's crossroads status is also unchanged, only it is trucks and diesel locomotives that crisscross the mountains here rather than canal boats and steam engines.

Cumberland is the county seat, a pristine historic town near the north branch of the Potomac. Though it was laid out by surveyor-Indian fighter Thomas Cresap before our Revolution, much of Cumberland is from the railroad boom days of the late

1800's. Washington Street was an elite residential address, and many of Cumberland's early homes were built by wealthy merchants. The entire city looks much as it did in 1875.

Tourism is becoming more and more important as Allegany County recognizes that its natural charm is a year-round attraction. Many come here to enjoy the beauty of the county's parks. There's hiking, biking, and swimming during the summer at Rocky Gap State Park, The Narrows, Dan Mountain State Park, and Green Ridge State Park. When the leaves are gone and the mountains are blanketed in snow the bicycles are put away in favor of skis and ice skates.

Many of the existing buildings and sites from Allegany's past are a visual reminder of the difficult life centuries ago in the Maryland mountains. An iron furnace still stands near Lonaconing, part of the county's manufacturing heritage. Cresap's House is a typical mountain home from the late 1700's, and the History House in Cumberland features several primitive rooms that testify to the hard life in the mountains.

Maryland's westernmost county, Garrett, corners the market on the largest, the highest, newest, and yes - coldest. Deep Creek Lake is Maryland's largest freshwater lake (and perhaps the state's second most popular vacation destination). Backbone Mountain is the state's highest at 3300 feet above sea level. Wisp is Maryland's largest ski area, and Garrett County itself is the state's newest at just over a century old.

Garrett County is a mountaintop playground. One-fifth of the county is public park land, lakes, and recreation areas. Visitors come to the rugged, pristinely-natural mountains all year around. In the summer there is hiking and water activities, and after the snow begins to fall there is skiing, snowmobiling, and all manner of winter sports.

Deep Creek Lake is the county's recreational focal point. The man-made lake was created when the Deep Creek Dam was completed in 1925. When the blue water is warm nearly every type of boat imaginable calls the lake home. Ice boats take over during the winter, and fishermen take walleye, yellow perch, and pike from beneath the ice. Nearby Swallow Falls State Parks boasts two breathtaking waterfalls. The river that flows through the rocky gorges here, the Youghiogheny, is a paradise for hikers and fishermen. Throughout the county there are numerous campsites, including the state's most beautiful primitive camping areas.

Garrett County's historic sites, however, reflect a period when there was little time for leisure. Pioneers began arriving here in the 1760's and the early settlers lived dangerous and difficult lives. They lived in log cabins and ate what they could grow during the short season, forage in the mountain glades, or hunt in the inhospitable forest. Major change did not come until the arrival of the railroad in 1851. The railroad brought markets for Garrett farmers and investors in timber and coal. Tourism began as a direct result of the iron horse. The B&O Railroad built several resort hotels in the late 1800's to give city-dwellers a reason to ride the trains to the Maryland mountains.

Modern Garrett County relies largely upon tourist revenues, as coal mining and forest industries have declined. Factories here turn out optical goods, clothing, and electronic equipment, but manufacturing provides a smaller percentage of total jobs than in any other county.

Western Maryland's tempestuous streams and rivers and ruggedly-beautiful mountains attract thousands from the rest of the state twelve months a year. This is an area of unsurpassed beauty which can provide a lifetime of woodland memories.

Near Uniontown, Carroll County

CARROLL COUNTY

Though it is for its rugged mountain landscape that western Maryland is best known, one begins to feel the pioneer spirit of the region in Carroll County. The county seat, Westminster, is the educational, political, cultural, and economic center of a rich and varied area.

Western Maryland College

Near Westminster, Carroll County

Uniontown

Nineteenth century farmhouse, Carroll County

UNIONTOWN

Uniontown, founded in 1802, captures the atmosphere of typical 19th century Carroll County small town life. It remains a quiet, peaceful one-street village with dozens of well-preserved homes.

WESTERN MARYLAND COLLEGE

Established in 1867, Western Maryland College was the first co-ed college founded south of the Mason-Dixon Line. From its hilltop perch, the college looks over old downtown Westminster.

Frederick County

FREDERICK COUNTY

By the time one reaches Frederick the foothills of the Appalachian Mountains are dimly visible to the west. Frederick County is the gateway to the Maryland mountains, and thousands come here every season to enjoy the county's many parks and recreation areas. At the same time, as Frederick County is discovered by Washingtonians, it is becoming more cosmopolitan. The pioneering spirit of early Western Marylanders helps to meet the needs of modern Frederick Countians.

New Market

NEW MARKET

New Market, in Frederick County, is the "Antiques Captial of Maryland". Dozens of shops line its Main Street, offering everything from vintage clothes to fine colonial furnishings.

Frederick County

Mother Seton Shrine

MOTHER SETON

Saint Elizabeth Ann Seton arrived in Frederick County in 1809, and shortly built the first parochial school in the nation. The work of this American-born saint is commemorated at several sites near Emmitsburg.

WASHINGTON COUNTY

Maryland's landscape graduates from rolling hills to breathtaking mountains in Washington County. Much of the past remains here—both physically and in spirit. Hagerstown, the county seat, is both an historical gem and an important business center. But it is the mountains that set the stage here, providing the basis for the county's economy as well as its geographic beauty and wealth of outdoor amenities.

SHARPSBURG, ANTIETAM NATIONAL BATTLEFIELD

The Civil War's bloodiest one-day battle shattered the silence of The Washington County farmlands, near Sharpsburg, in 1862. Monuments fill the quiet fields in memory of the thousands who fell here.

Washington County

Allegany County

ALLEGANY COUNTY

Throughout the nineteenth century Allegany County was a crossroads, where railroad, highway, and canals met. George Washington was among its earliest surveyors and our first President would still recognize much in this mountainous county. Allegany boasts an impressive park system, many significant historic sites, and a strong cultural movement.

Cumberland

CUMBERLAND

Located on the old National Road, Cumberland played host to thousands who passed through here on their way west. The town is a wealth of early architecture, much dating from the middle 1800's.

West of Deep Creek Lake, Garrett County

GARRETT COUNTY

The westernmost county, as well as Maryland's least densely populated, Garrett County bills itself as a vacation wonderland. There are many reasons to come to Garrett County - breathtaking waterfalls, unsurpassed fishing, and skiing that can match any in the Mid-Atlantic states. Many have found that Garrett County is not only a great vacation spot, but also a pretty good place to live and work.

Savage River State Forest

SAVAGE RIVER STATE FOREST

With 53,000 acres of trees, streams, and wildlife, the Savage River State Forest is Maryland's largest woodland preserve. There are fine camping facilities here as well as excellent fishing and hunting along the swift-flowing Savage River.

Deep Creek Lake

DEEP CREEK LAKE

Deep Creek Lake is the largest freshwater lake in the state. During summer months, nearly every type of boat from sailboat to speedster can be seen on its clear blue waters.

Muddy Creek Falls

Garrett County

Deep Creek Lake

Swallow Falls

MUDDY CREEK FALLS

At 64 feet, Muddy Creek Falls is the largest waterfall in Maryland, set in a forest of stunning natural beauty. The falls are framed by tall slopes covered by giant hemlock trees.

SWALLOW FALLS

The centerpiece of Garrett State Forest is Swallow Falls, if not the biggest, undeniably the most beautiful waterfalls in the state. Nearby Herrington Manor State Park offers camping and many outdoor activities.

MARYLAND PORT ADMINISTRATION

    Under the management of the Maryland Port Administration, which has overseen shipping in the state for over thirty years, the Port of Baltimore has kept pace with the demands of international trade. The centerpiece of its work is the Dundalk Marine Terminal, a modern facility in which the Port Administration has invested over $200 million in the past twenty years.

MARYLAND'S ECONOMY

Three centuries ago the Maryland economy, like that of all of her sister colonies, was linked fast to soil and water. The rivers that made their way to the Chesapeake were the major routes of trade, and Maryland was virtually isolated from the other English settlements. Philadelphia was a dusty, rigorous two-day ride and Washington was a hundred years in the future.

Although modern Maryland bears scarcely any economic resemblance at all to her roots, they are still there if one but scratches the surface. It is hard to imagine a state that could have changed as much and yet remained so much the same. The economy is grounded in high technology and services, international trade, and a constantly-changing manufacturing base. Professional and technical workers make up over a fifth of the state's work force, the highest percentage of any state in the nation.

Yet many Marylanders still turn to the land or the water for their livelihoods. Generation after generation of watermen have taken their small wooden boats across the Bay in search of crabs, oysters, clams, and fin fish and the likelihood that the activity will continue indefinitely is indisputable. Granted, many oystermen dive for the succulent shellfish instead of dredging or tonging as their fathers did. But the tradition remains. In Southern Maryland tobacco is still king in many respects, and the fields of central Maryland still produce wheat and truck produce as they have since the first settler arrived there.

What cannot be ignored is the new relationship between Maryland and the rest of the East Coast. Baltimore is in the very center of the busy Atlanta-Boston corridor, and a major hub of commercial transportation. Maryland was the birthplace of modern railroading, and Conrail and the CSX Corporation still serve the state and the entire Atlantic seaboard. Both freight and passenger rail service is excellent. Major interstate highways slice the state north-to-south and east-to-west, permanently linking the state economy with that of her neighbors.

The Port of Baltimore, with 45 miles of renewed waterfront, can handle 200 ships at a time. Its piers are constantly filled with vessels flying hundreds of international standards. Three major airports serve Maryland residents and visitors, making Maryland the nation's fourth largest air travel market.

All this adds up to general prosperity for Marylanders. The average Maryland household income is 10% higher than the national average and the unemployment rate is usually two points below that of the entire nation.

Certainly patterns of employment are rapidly changing. Manufacturing jobs are declining in many sectors, especially heavy basic industries. The coal industry of the Maryland mountains employs but a small fraction of the work force of just fifty years ago. Canning on the Eastern Shore is not the industry it was at the turn of the century. Yet there have always been enough new opportunities to help fill the gap. The boom in the service sector, especially in tourist-related businesses in Baltimore and western Maryland, has provided jobs that didn't exist just a decade ago. Even more important is the growth of high technology. Of the ten largest state employers, six are involved in some aspect of high-tech work.

The state's adaptability to a changing economic environment has not come without cooperation between the private sector and the state government. Maryland's financial assistance programs have helped new businesses get off the ground as well as providing aid in the growth of long-standing concerns. Maryland has been a pioneer in establishing enterprise zones that offer various packages of economic incentives and tax advantages to growing businesses and those that choose to move to the state. Coupled with the state's three foreign trade zones, the climate for business growth is constantly improving.

All these are among the reasons why so many business have decided to make Maryland their home. But there's also the hospitable climate, diverse cultural and recreational attractions, a fine network of educational institutions, and a proximity to Washington, Philadelphia and New York. Coupled with a stable economy and the resulting job opportunities, the state of Maryland has much to offer its resident businesses.

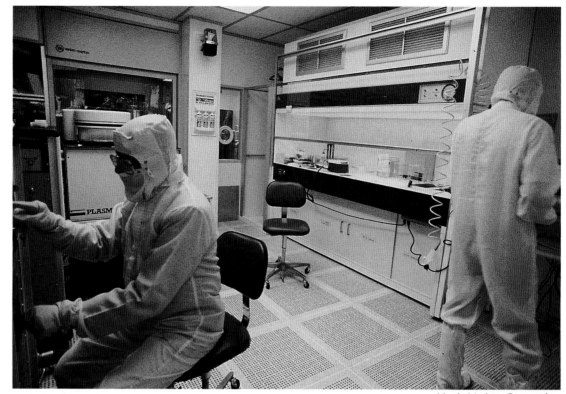

Whitney, Bailey, Cox and Magnani

Martin Marietta Corporation

The Chesapeake and Potomac Telephone Company

Scheer Partners, Inc.

WHITNEY, BAILEY, COX, AND MAGNANI

WBCM has helped turn visions to reality for Maryland on such projects as the Space Telescope Science Institute and sections of the new Interstate 195 which connects BWI Airport to Interstate 95. A consulting engineering firm specializing in highways and bridges, marine and sanitary/environmental projects, building structures, site planning and landscape architecture. WBCM has been an important force in Maryland's renaissance.

THE CHESAPEAKE AND POTOMAC TELEPHONE COMPANY

C&P Telephone provides telephone service to more than 700,000 customers throughout the Baltimore metropolitan area. Advanced communications and data transmission systems give C&P a high level of reliability in connecting Baltimore businesses and residents with the rest of the world.

MARTIN MARIETTA CORPORATION

An aerospace, electronics, and information technology company, Martin Marietta Corporation's Aero & Naval Systems operation in Middle River features engineering and precision manufacturing technology for defense systems. Martin Marietta Laboratories, in Catonsville, is the corporation's research center. The huge B-26 Marauder bomber once rolled off Martin Marietta's Baltimore assembly lines, but today's technological challenges are found in microelectronic circuits that are smaller than a single particle of dust.

SCHEER PARTNERS, INC.

Scheer Partners is a full service commercial real estate firm specializing in the needs of the Maryland business community, with professional experts in office leasing, land development, investment acquisition and property management. Scheer Partners offers a full complement of real estate services to its clients.

Crown Central Petroleum

CROWN CENTRAL PETROLEUM CORPORATION
The only oil company headquartered in Maryland, Crown Central Petroleum Corporation is a major distributor of petroleum products throughout the state and the Mid-Atlantic Southeastern region. The company's numerous clean, efficient retail outlets throughout the area are supplied from its major terminal and storage facility in Baltimore. With gross sales in excess of $1 billion, this Fortune 500 corporation is one of the largest companies headquartered in Baltimore. Crown is a long-time supporter of community activities in the city and state.

O'CONOR, PIPER, & FLYNN

Since 1984, O'Conor, Piper and Flynn has been the leading locally-owned real estate company in Maryland. With 40 offices specializing in residential, commercial/industrial, and investment real estate, the firm continues to grow, with annual sales of over $1 billion. O'Conor, Piper and Flynn is a full service real estate company, and is recognized for innovative marketing and respected for its hundreds of years of combined industry experience.

GENERAL MOTORS

The General Motors Truck and Bus Assembly Plant in Baltimore is one of the most modern facilities of its type in the country. Currently employing 4,000 people, the plant produces over 200,000 midsized vans annually, and will soon produce its 10 millionth vehicle since production began in March, 1935.

BALTIMORE GAS AND ELECTRIC

Baltimore Gas and Electric Company is an investor-owned utility engaged in the production and sales of electricity and the sales of natural gas. BG&E has a long tradition of quality service, providing energy to well over two million Maryland residents. Its Calvert Cliffs Nuclear Plant, ranking as one of the top-performing nuclear facilities in the nation, is one of ten BG&E electric generating plants in the state.

T. ROWE PRICE ASSOCIATES

For over half a century, T. Rowe Price Associates has provided high-quality investment management services to all types of investors. They are investment counselors to institutions, endowments, trusts, foundations, and individuals, as well as advisor to the T. Rowe Price family of no-load mutual funds. They are managers for over 20 billion in assets and maintain a specialized, decentralized approach to investment management.

THE RYLAND GROUP

Based in Columbia, Maryland, Ryland is known in 17 states coast to coast as one of the largest home builders in the nation. Since 1967, more than 70,000 families have found a home in Ryland. But Ryland boasts a record of building more than homes. The company is also recognized for its strong standing in the mortgage banking and modular home building fields.

MARYLAND NATIONAL BANK

Maryland National Bank has grown from its start in 1933 to the state's largest commercial banking organization, with assets of over $8 billion. It offers full range of banking services at branches throughout Maryland as well as overseas branches in the Bahamas, Europe, the Far East, and South America.

W.R. GRACE & CO. DAVISON CHEMICAL DIVISION

Founded and headquartered in Baltimore in 1832, the W.R Grace & Co. Davison Chemical Division has established a world wide reputation for quality specialty chemicals and innovative product and application technology. Almost 800 of the 2,000 men and women in this division are employed at the Curtis Bay Maryland manufacturing complex.

AAI CORPORATION

With offices and manufacturing facilities on a 90-acre tract in Hunt Valley, AAI Corporation carries out systems development and production primarily for the Department of Defense. Equipment built here covers the entire spectrum of weapons systems training and testing, while ordnance programs concentrate on advanced development of armored vehicles, munitions, and weapons. Organized in 1950, AAI continues to be a world leader in defense products.

Point Lookout, St. Mary's County